# THE CHANGIN

# Witney

## BOOK ONE

## Derek Honey

Robert Boyd
PUBLICATIONS

Published by
*Robert Boyd Publications*
260 Colwell Drive
Witney, Oxfordshire OX8 7LW

First published 1998

Copyright © Derek Honey and
*Robert Boyd Publications*

ISBN: 1 899536 31 0

## OTHER TITLES IN THE *CHANGING FACES* SERIES

Banbury: Book One
Bicester: Book One
Bladon with Church Hanborough and
    Long Hanborough
Botley and North Hinksey
Cowley
Cowley: Book Two
Cowley Works: Book One
Cumnor and Appleton with Farmoor
    and Eaton
St Clements and East Oxford:
    Book One
St Clements and East Oxford:
    Book Two
Eynsham: Book One
Eynsham: Book Two
Headington: Book One
Headington: Book Two
Jericho: Book One
Littlemore and Sandford
Marston: Book One
Marston: Book Two
North Oxford: Book One

North Oxford: Book Two
Oxford City Centre: Book One
South Oxford: Book One
Summertown and Cutteslowe
St Ebbes and St Thomas: Book One
St Ebbes and St Thomas: Book Two
West Oxford
Wolvercote with Wytham and Godstow
Woodstock: Book One
Woodstock: Book Two

### FORTHCOMING

Abingdon
Banbury: Book Two
Bicester: Book Two
Chipping Norton
Cowley: Book Three
Faringdon and District
Grimsbury
Jericho: Book Two
Kennington
Thame
Yarnton and Begbroke with Cassington

Printed and bound in Great Britain at The Alden Press, Oxford

# Contents

---

### Front cover photograph

Children celebrating the end of war in 1945 with a street party in West End.

### Back cover photograph

This view of the High Street, taken about 1903, is noted for the absence of traffic. What horse traffic there is, Walter Midwinter's cab can be seen in the foreground, seems to have little regard for the rules of the road — most of it appears to be driving on the right hand side of the road — the one cart outside the Temperance Hotel obeying the rules. Behind the trees to the left was the Post Office, now Denton's shop, while opposite the Temperance Hotel remains much the same and is now Boots store.

# Acknowledgements

The author wishes to thank the many schools, companies, librarians and individuals, who through their kindness have made this book possible.

The Centre for Oxfordshire Studies, Witney Library, Bodleian Library, Henry Box School, the Witney Museum and Art Gallery, the Oxford Mail, Witney Gazette and the archives of Courage Ltd.

I am particularly grateful to the following people for their help on certain chapters.

Brian Crawford of the Blanket Hall for allowing me access to the Early family photographic archives. To Ruth Edy and Mary Perry of Henry Box School and the Headteacher Mr D.R. Walker for permission to reproduce the two school crests. I am also grateful to Stanley Jenkins of the Witney Museum for his expert knowledge on the Witney Railway and his source material on Clinch's Brewery. Also to Michael Druce for his help on Saltmarsh and Druce and the Witney bombs, and to Cyril Godfrey and the Witney Fire Brigade.

Those who have also provided photographs include: Barry Allen, Percy Brown, John Chiperfield, Eddie Calcutt, John Dossett-Davies, Ted Hare, Freda Horne, Leo Hicks, Bill Simpson, Brian James, Catherine Taylor and Arthur Titherington.

My thanks goes to them all. While every effort is made to ensure correct identification of those appearing in the photographs, the occasional error is inevitable when relying on human memory.

# Introduction

In 969, King Edgar signed a charter giving land at Wyttange in the Wychwood Forest to the Saxon chief, Oelfnelm. At this time it was no bigger than a hamlet in the area that is now Corn Street. Strategically the settlement controlled the dyke over a stream that lead westward on the pilgrims route to Glastonbury. By 1044 it had reverted back to the crown and Edward the Confessor granted the land to Alfwine the Bishop of Winchester, and this is the first record of the town's long association with the See of Winchester. It was Bishop Stigand (1047-70) who began to build a palace on its present site at Church Green. In the Domesday Book of 1086, the settlement, then known as Witenie, was recorded as having 300 persons.

During the civil war between King Steven and Empress Matilda (1135-50) the palace was fortified by Bishop Henry de Blois, the brother of Steven, who changed sides when Steven refused to make him Archbishop of Canterbury. But it was under Bishop Peter des Roches (1205-38) that the town started to prosper as a centre for cloth making. By time of King John, Witney had become an important town, and John – who was born at Woodstock – made several visits between 1207 and 1214. His son, Henry III who succeeded to the throne as a teenager, visited Witney in 1221 and ordered a suit of clothing for the sum of 30 Marks (£20). By 1279 the population numbered over one thousand persons, but this was reduced by a third when the Black Death struck the area in 1348.

The Bishops played a big part in the development of the town, a connection that lasted through to the middle of the 19th Century, with only two breaks. Bishop John Ponet gave back the land to Edward VI in 1551, but it was returned to the See only seven years later. While during the period of the Commonwealth the town was given to William Lenthall, the Speaker of the House of Commons, who lived at Burford. On the restoration of Charles II the land reverted back to the church.

Since the end of the 14th Century much of the land was leased out to various tenants, including Lord Cornbury in 1670, and later to Edward Hyde, the Earl of Clarendon. In 1751 the town and surrounding land was leased out to the Duke of Marlborough and his descendants bought the manor outright in 1862, bring the Winchester connection to an end.

Blanket and clothmaking have been the foundation of Witney's prosperity since the 13th Century, but it was not until 1711 that Queen Anne – the granddaughter of the Earl of Clarendon – granted the Master Weavers their own Royal Charter of Incorporation. The foremost families being the Colliers, the Marriots and the Earlys. During the middle of the 19th Century, William Smith converted his White Hart Brewery into a blanket mill after first making mops, and was the first to use steam power to run the factory. While during the early part of the 20th Century, Walkers of Mirfield in Yorkshire moved to the town setting up a mill at the Crofts. Now only Earlys remain in the town, sited in a new mill on the Burford Road, although it is no longer owned by the family.

Witney High Street, 1905.

The English Civil War between the Crown and Parliament had very little impact on the town, although King Charles did stay for three nights on 18th-20th June 1644, at the White Hart Inn — now part of the Bridge Street Industrial Estate. Cromwell also visited the town in 1649 while on his way to Burford. During the First War World many of Witney's young men volunteered and 157 did not return, while the town played host to many foreigners. Belgian and Polish refugees were billeted in and around Witney, including in the old Workhouse on Tower Hill. In 1918 the town was 'invaded' by American and Canadian servicemen. They even ran their own baseball league on the Leys playing field. During the Second World War, Witney lost 35 men and their names and their First World War comrades are commemorated on the War Memorial on Church Green. Only two bombs were dropped on Witney, neither doing much damage, but part of the crater of one can still be seen outside St Mary's School on Church Green. Witney airfield, owned by de Havilland — now Bromag's Industrial Estate — made an important contribution to the war effort, repairing and rebuilding planes, while parachutes were assembled in a factory on the Leys — now Poundstretchers. During the Second World War until the 1960s the town was again visited by American servicemen who were stationed at RAF Brize Norton.

Witney has grown considerably in the past few years, new housing estates being built on open-field land on the outskirts, and the population is now over 20,000 — with plans for even more. To compensate for this new shopping centres have been built in the town, with four supermarkets. The town has a lively social life, with numerous activities, a leisure centre, a cinema (in the Corn Exchange), a nightclub, regular dances in the Langdale Hall, two snooker halls, its own football team in a new stadium on Downs Road, various restaurants and 23 pubs. Car parking is free throughout the town and the streets reasonably safe at night. Oxford and London are close, with regular buses to both places. Despite this, it remains still a pleasant market town with a deep sense of its own history.

# THE PALACE WITNEY

## THE HOUSE OF PERFECT SOUND.

Telephone:—Witney 147.

**To-night and Saturday**

WHEELER and WOOLSEY in

# SO THIS IS AFRICA

A Riot of Fun. Also

# NATURES WORKSHOP

**Next Monday, Tuesday and Wednesday**

EDNA MAY OLIVER and ROBERT ARMSTRONG in

# The Penguin Pool Mystery

also WILLIAM FRESHMAN in

# LUCKY BLAZE

**Next Thursday, Friday and Saturday**

CHARLIE MURRAY and GEORGE SIDNEY in

# THE COHENS and KELLYS in TROUBLE

Mickey Mouse presents **"MICKEY'S MELLERDAMA."**

Times of Showing—Saturday 5-30 till 10. Other days 6 till 10 15.
Afternoons—Thursday and Saturday at 2 o'clock.
Prices of Admission Including Tax.—Balcony, 2/4 and 1/10. Ground Floor. 1/6, 1/3. 1/- and 8d

Advert for the Palace Cinema in the *Witney Gazzette,* Friday 20th July 1934.

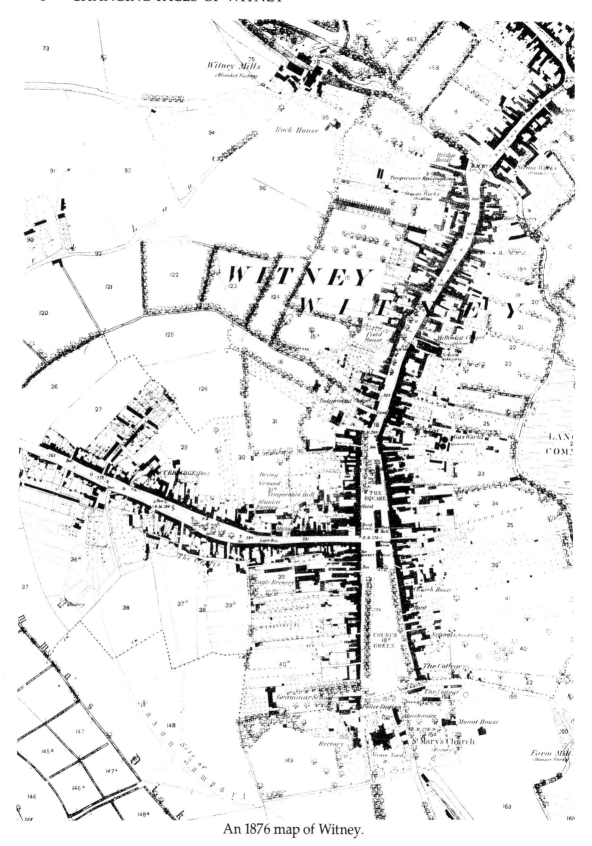

An 1876 map of Witney.

SECTION ONE

# Earlys of Witney

Since the Thirteenth Century the making of cloth has played an important part in the town's development. Starting off as a cottage industry, by the Seventeenth Century large mills began to develop. One of the first and now the only blanket mill in the town belonged to the Early Family. In 1669 Richard Early sold woollen stockings in Corn Street, and he apprenticed his son Thomas to Mr Silman a blanketmaker. He inherited the business and by the time James II visited Witney in 1688 it was Thomas who presented the king with a pair of gold-fringed blankets. Since then until recently the family have lived and worked where the firm is based now — over eight generations. It is also one of the two oldest companies in the country to trade throughout its business life in the same line — making blankets. It has deep royal connections having made blankets for Charles II in 1688 and has supplied fifteen monarchs as well as holding a Royal Warrant under thirteen successive Kings and Queens. From 1711 under Queen Anne through to the present Queen Elizabeth II.

All the blanketmakers of Witney used the wool from the local sheep, large, woolly animals nicknamed Cotswold Lions, because of their size. A wide variety of fabrics were made from it, including 'duffields' which was woven into pieces 30 yards long and 1 yards wide, then dyed red and blue. These colours particularly found favour with North American Indians who traded fur for them for use as clothing. A special point system was devised, the number of coloured stripes woven indicating the number of furs or skins to be traded. Other products made were hammocks for sailors, tilt cloths used as covers for the loads on barges and later mops for the Royal Navy.

From their original Quaker roots through to Methodism, the Early family have always played a major part in the welfare of Witney. The firm operated one of the first profit sharing schemes, helped with the education of local children, encouraged alcoholic abstinence — although Joseph Early owned the Blanket Hall Brewery during the mid-1800s which was financed by his father Edward — and provided housing for their workers. The Earlys have always been at the forefront of new developments. In 1800 the flying-shuttle loom was introduced — not without opposition from their workers — and in 1818 John Early introduced spinning machines.

Unlike many woollen towns in the Nineteenth Century, Witney continued to prosper, mainly due to most of the larger blanketmakers being related, thus helping each other out. The Earlys were related by marriage to the Marriotts and the Vanners, and Edward Early financed the education of William Smith, the owner of another large mill in the town, and once employed him as an inspector.

By the Twentieth Century wool was imported to Witney from all over the world and the final product exported back, the Jacquard fabrics with their strong figured patterns were popular in South America and South Africa.

The Earlys became the most influential family in Witney. They also married into the family of Lord Heyter. Charles Early — who was one of the original backers of the

John Early 1706-1795

Witney Railway Company — lived at Newland House on Oxford Hill, close to his warehouse. The family also had homes on Woodgreen, East End and the High Street. They set up numerous charity benefits for the town, educated poor children, were magistrates, set up the Coffee Tavern — a non-alcoholic pub now Boots store — and built and provided houses for their workers. Blankets are still made at Earlys, mainly cellular for hospitals — and its Earlywarm blankets are famous throughout the world, but although the company is no longer owned by the family, high quality is still the keynote. The new management realise customers now require fashionable products to compliment their whole bedroom decor, so design has become a third dimension complementing the complete bed.

Early family group taken in the grounds of Newland House in 1879.

1: Charles William Early (1850-1943) 2: Martha Naomi nee Dolton (1851-1935) 3: Sarah Early nee Vanner (1824-1906) 4: Charles Early (1824-1912) 5: Mrs J.E.Vanner (1826-1905) 6: Sarah Heyter Chubb nee Vanner Early 7: Charles Chubb (1871-1967) 8: George Chubb (1875-1957) 9: ? could be Charles Early's brother. 10: Annie Early nee Cole (1856-1939) 11: James Vanner Early (1853-1920) 12: Thomas Cole 13: George Hayter Cubb (1848-1946?) 14: James Engelbert Vanner (1834-1906)

The Tuckers had one of the hardest jobs at the mill, with the result they gained an elitists reputation in the town. At the mill they were responsible for hanging out blankets in loops on wooden rods. Yellow rock sulphur was placed in cast iron trays, the sulphur was lit, the house closed and left overnight for the blankets to bleach. The Tuckers were also responsible for setting the stockfuls out to dry on the tenter hooks — prior to bleaching.

One of the highlights of the Tuckers' year was the annual Tuckers' Feast. Originally held in the Blanket Hall where the men received their fees for the year, they often turned out to be a long, somewhat boozy affairs. It was traditional the Tuckers were presented with a clay pipe and a bowlful of tobacco.

Tuckers outside the Sulphur House in 1898. Left to right, back row: Alf Basson, Thomas Teagle, ?, Jim Brooks, Eli Miles. Middle row: 'Massa' Keates, Charles Keates, Bill Hickman, C. Weaver, Joe Winfield, Jimmy Martin. Front row: Bill Hosier, Tom Wiggins, Bill Miles.

The Tuckers' Feast held on 1 March 1960, left to right: Bert Coles, Dennis Smith, ?, Sid Harlow.

Tuckers Feast 1960. Left to right: Tom Hathaway, George Smith, E.J.Warner, Mr Lock, Herbet Smith.

The Shed Men in 1929. Left to right: Daniel Fidler, Herbert Woodcock, Fred Gould, Jack Hill, Alfred Sessions, Reg Paister, Albert Pratley, Albert Moss, Stan Allen, Harold Warner, W.A.Parr (Foreman).

On 2 October 1956 Earlys presented Tom Leigh, Chairman of the Witney Urban District Council, with a new chain of office in the Council Chambers at 26 Church Green. The reception was held later in the Fleece Hotel.

The men prominent in the photograph at the Fleece Hotel are, left to right: Dudley Hopkins, Tom Leigh, Charles Micklewright, Harold Early, E.S. (Chunky) Woods, Patrick Early.

Burford Road Estate in 1929.

In 1926 Earlys set up the Witney Mills Housing Association to provide housing for their workers on the Burford Road and Springfield Estate. The first 20 houses were built in 1929 but there were not enough employees to take up the offer or could not afford the 5/- a week rent. So some of the houses were let to outsiders.

Staff from Earlys setting off on a trip to the seaside on 20 April 1959.

1 Mrs Abbott 2 H. Abbott 3 W. Beale 4 W. Wardell 5 Miss Wardell 6 Master Wardell 7 Mrs Wardell 8 R. Jennings 9 Mrs Keates 10 Andy Maynard 11 G. Maynard 12 Miss Buckingham 13 Mrs Maynard 14 Miss W. Davies 15 Master Davies 16 Will Hayley 19 Mrs W. Beale 20 Miss G. Haley 21 G.Baker 22 Mrs R. Painter 23 R. Painter 24 L. Goddard 25 Miss C. Pratley 26 R. Pratley 27 Miss L. Goddard 28 Master Goddard 29 Mrs R. Pratley 30 Miss J. Keates 31 J. Keates 32 Miss R. Bowells 33 Miss J. Bowells.

Preparing lunch for the workers in 1940. Left to right: ?, Evelyn Lock, ?, Dorothy Bolton, Miss Cheryl.

Many of the workers at Earlys started straight from school and remained there the rest of their lives. In 1949 Earlys set up their Half-century Club for workers who had worked at the mill for fifty years or more.

The first meeting of the Half-century Club held in August 1949. With J.H. Early are left to right: Mary Haley, Sarah Clack, Alice Clack.

Another meeting of the Half-century Club held at Riverside Gardens in 1951. Left to right: William Haley, Harold Early, Tom Hicks, Arthur Parr, Will Hedges, Ernest Haley, Frank Gribber.

Early's workers ran several sports clubs. One of the most popular was bowls. The Green was at Riverside Gardens in Mill Street.

Bowls match held in 1957 at Riverside. The houses to the rear are Mill Street Cottages. Those featured are: Beszard Room (hands in pockets), Will Hedges (holding pipe), George Pumfrey, Bill Blake (behind bowl).

Another sporting pastime was football and Witney Mills F.C. won several trophies in their day.

Witney Mills FC winners of Junior Challenge Cup 1959  Back row, left to right: Harold Radbone, Norman Clapton, Charlie Haley, ?, Ian Paton, ?, Adrian Horne, Brian Moynes. Front row: Douglas Allen, ?, Ken Craske (Capt), ?, Charlie Fisher.

Witney Mills Cricket Club and their ground at Newlands were famous throughout the county. G.W. Grace actually played in an invitation match there at the end of the last century.

Witney Mills Cricket Club 1934 Back row, left to right: Norman Waite, Maurice Fyfield, Harold Cooper, Fred Strange, Tom Pearson. Front Row: Cyril Nunn, Tom Scarsbrook, Bernard Middleton, Stanley Bridgeman (Capt), Bernard Room, Percy Hosier, Richard Early.

On 8 June 1906, Earlys decided to challenge the record of Sir John Throckmorton of Buckland, who, for a bet of 1,000 guineas, took wool from his Southdown sheep, had cloth woven and a coat made in thirteen hours twenty minutes. The shearing began at 3.46 am, the weaving began at 8.10 am, and ended when the tuckers began washing, shrinking, dying and raising the nap. The blankets were finished at 2.23pm, a total of ten hours thirty-seven minutes. The blankets were presented and used the same night by the Duke of Marlborough.

Shearing sheep on 8 June 1906 at New Mill for the record of making a pair of blankets in under 11 hours

At the turn of the 18th Century, Earlys along with other blanketmakers in Witney applied to Queen Anne for a Royal Charter of Incorporation to protect their name. This was granted in 1711 and on August 10th they held their first meeting at Staple Hall. By 1720 they decided to build their own hall, and purchased from John Butler his pub in the High Street. Rebuilt by December 1721 the hall was used for social events was well as for business. In 1844 Edward Early bought the Hall and leased it out to his son Joseph and William Smith who set up the Blanket Hall Brewery. William soon left to start his own brewery and in 1869 Joseph sold out to the Shillingford Brothers, before emigrating to Australia. Arthur Bateman bought the brewery in 1881 and in 1890 it was bought by Clinch's Brewery. The Hall with its famous one-handed clock was, during the Second World War, a mineral water factory and is now a private house, owned by a former member of staff at Earlys.

The Blanket Hall in the High Street.

During its lifetime Early's mill has seen many royal visits. The most notable during the Twentieth Century being Queen Mary the last Queen Mother on Thursday 8 August 1941, and the Present Queen on 8 April 1959.

The visit of Queen Mary. Left to right: J. Harold Early, H.M. Queen Mary, Ernest Haley, Herbert Beale (wearing smock).

The visit of H.M. Queen Elizabeth II. Left to right: Jimmy Hill, Charlie Fisher, HRH Queen Earl of Macclesfield, J.F. Early, Brian Crawford.

# *Saltmarsh and Druce*

This family grocers was established at 44, Market Square by Messrs Saltmarsh and Druce in 1873, and has remained in the same premises since. One of the oldest established shops in Witney it was initially leased from Leigh's next door but towards the end of the century the freehold of the premises were bought. Then known as the Tea Market, since that time it has changed very little. There are no long queues at cash check-outs, trolleys or saver cards, it remains a country shop where assistants are still there to give the customer personal service. Freshly ground coffee gives an aromatic smell and individual cuts of meat and cheese are still served. Recently a small coffee shop was placed to the rear of the premises. In 1897 the shop produced a price list of his goods, which is an almanac for Witney. Members of Parliament, Councillors, Courts, Bailiffs, various societies, sporting organisations, churches and Post Office and railway times were all quoted. Then the shop not only sold groceries and beverages — alcoholic or otherwise — but brooms and brushes, fruit, disinfectants, candles, medicines, and perfumes. Customers had a choice of payment, either by cash or credit for which a small charge was made, but by spending over £1 delivery was free. The shop even had its own representatives in the villages to take orders. The present owner, Michael Druce, is the grandson of one of the founders. Apart from its extensive retail trade, despite the presence of supermarkets in the town, it also has a wholesale warehouse to the rear of Market Square.

Saltmarsh and Druce shop assistants about 1920.

Letterhead of 1924.

One of the first company representative cars about mid-nineteen twenties.

An early Saltmarsh and Druce representive's business card.

## LOCAL INFORMATION.
### 1897.

**Members of Parliament for Oxfordshire.**

SOUTH—Harman Hodge, Esq., *Conservative.*   MID—G. H. Morrell, Esq., *Conservative.*
NORTH—A. Brassey, Esq., *Conservative.*

**County Councillors.**

Witney: W. Smith; Hailey: J. V. Early; Stanlake: A. Blake; Burford: J. Jacobs; Broadwell: W. H. Fox; Bampton: P. Southby; Eynsham: C. Watts.

**WITNEY.**

**Urban District Council.**

*Chairman:*—J. Knight.

| RETIRE MARCH, 1899. | RETIRE MARCH, 1900. | RETIRE MARCH, 1898. |
| --- | --- | --- |
| C. Gerring | I. Dingle | J. Clarke |
| C. Viner | H. Middleton | A. Merritt |
| J. Knight | J. Brunton | |
| *Surveyor*— Graham. | | *Collector*—H. J Merchant |

*Clerk*—F. J. D. Westell.   *Deputy Coroner*—F. J. D. Westell.
*Lord of the Manor*—The Duke of Marlborough.
*Steward of the Manor* F. J. D. Westell.
*Coroner*—F. Westell.

*Court of Petty Sessions.*—MAGISTRATES-Rev. R. L. Baker (Chairman); Captain Wynter; Ransden: J. Mason, Esq., Eynsham Hall; J. F. Mason, Esq., Freeland Lodge; Philip Soothby and J. F. Staple-Browne, Esqs., Bampton; C. Early, C. D. Batt, W. Smith and R. Raikes, Esq.s. Witney. CLERK-H T. Ravenor. SUPERINTENDENT OF POLICE—Jos Cook. SERGEANT—H. Dickenson. Sittings at the Justice Room every alternate Thursday.

*County Court*—JUDGE—T. W. Snagge, Esq., Q.C. REGISTRAR AND HIGH BAILIFF—F. J. D. Westell. Court BAILIFF—T. Andrews. SITTINGS—Bi-monthly.

*Poor Law Union*—Chairman: Rev. R. L. Baker; Vice-Chairman: Mr. John Nalder; Guardians for Witney: S. Shuffrey, Rev. J. Brantom and Mrs. C. W. Early; Ex-Officio: W. Smith, Hailey: Harry Robbins and E. A. Blake, Curbridge; J. D. Bliss, Crawley; W. H. Cook. Rev. E. J. U. Payne. Chaplain: N. J. G. Ravenor, Clerk: W. J. Clarke, Master of the Workhouse; James Merchant. Relieving Officer. Day of Guardians Meeting—Thursday.

*Rural District Council*—Chairman: Rev. R. L. Baker; Vice-Chairman: Mr. J. Nalder; All members of the Council are also Guardians for their parishes. N. J. G. Ravenor, Clerk; W. Fyson, Wood, M.D., 50, St. John Street, Oxford, Medical Officer of Health; W. G. Eaton, Inspector of Nuisances, Wood Green, G. Wallis, Surveyor, Bampton.

*Bailiffs*—O. D. Batt and W. H. Tarrant, Junr.
*Assistant Overseer*—H. J. Merchant.
*Superintendent Registrar*—N. J. G. Ravenor.

*Choral Society*—Presidents: C. D. Batt and J. V. Early, Esq's. Secretaries: Messrs. W. H. Tarrant. Jun., and W. T. Felton. Committee: Messrs. A. C. Bateman, G. Dyke, C. Gerring, F. M. Green. F. Hayter, A. L. Leigh, J. C. Sims, E. Tarrant, J. Verney, F. S. Walter and H. W. Young. Conductor: G. Owens.

Saltmarsh and Druce advert and a 'local information' page from their price list of 1897.

A photograph taken between 1887-95 of Market Square showing the first Saltmarsh and Druce delivery cart.

Half a century later Arthur Harding standing by his delivery van.

More up-to-date transport in 1960.

# Henry Box School
## Formerly Witney Grammar School

Left: The original school crest

Right: the present school crest.

Founded by Henry and Mary Box in 1660, until 1908 the Box Building alone housed the school. As well as the school-room, it also provided accommodation for the Master, the Usher and boarders. The original school house remains. Until 1902 the Grocers' Company — of which Henry Box was a member — were the Governers of the school and appointed the Masters and staff. Priority was given to the sons of Witney, but could also include Hailey, Crawley and Curbridge. Its main function was to teach Latin, Greek and Hebrew for it was assumed they could already read.

Since 1902, the school was part aided by the County and in 1939 the Governers leased the school to the County as a maintained school under the Articles of Government. The last headmaster to live in the school was Basil Robinson and it was he who converted the school-room into a library in 1959.

In the year of the school's tercentenary, on Wednesday 20th July 1960, the school was honoured with a visit from H.M. Elizabeth the Queen Mother, who landed on Church Green in a helicopter of the Queen's Flight. She was greeted by Earl Macclesfield, Lord Lieutenant of Oxfordshire; The High Sheriff of Oxfordshire, Col H.W. Morrell; The Lord Bishop of Oxford, Harry Carpenter; Neil Marten MP; Mr R.E. Tarrant, Chairman Witney Urban District Council; and the Chief Constable of Oxfordshire, Mr J.Bailey. Also present was the headmaster Mr Robinson, the Governors of the school and members of the staff and pupils.

Her Majesty then formally opened the new library, the New Buildings, the Memorial Pavilon and the Hard Tennis Courts. Afterwards the Lord Bishop of Oxford Harry Carpenter dedicated the New Buildings.

As the school expanded during the 1970s the school outgrew this location for the library but it was not until 1992 the refurbishment of the original building was authorised, and this was reopened in April 1994 by Rt. Hon. Douglas Hurd MP, the then Foreign Secretary.

Now one of two secondary schools in Witney, the other being Wood Green, it has maintained a high level of academic ability and well as several notable sporting and social achievements.

James Harold Early. Chairman of Governors 1924-55.

On May 31, 1760 a petition was sent by the town to the Grocers' Company in London for the dismissal of the writing teacher Stephen Day and for the appointment of his replacement Mr Wright.

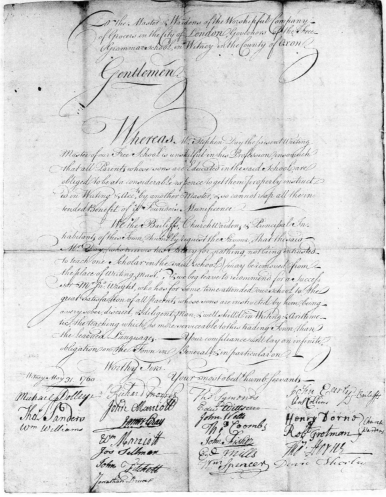

Staff in 1955, back row: Mr McGregor, Mr Thompson(?), Mr Ford, Mrs Clennell, Mr Faulkner. Front row: Mr Singer, Miss Spencer, Mr Edwards, Mr Robinson (Head), Mrs Hemmings, Mr Causer, Miss Therman.

The library in the 1970s.

Girls Hockey Team 1968, winners of Junior County Hockey Tournament. Back row: Mrs Comb, Angela Brogden, Christine Bridgewater, Margaret Hopley, Sandra Smith, Elizabeth Edens. Front row: M. Hodge, Winifred Hanson(?), Marjorie Simity(?), Yvonne Castle, Elizabeth Williamson, Anita O'Brien.

Drama has always played a large part in the school activities. A production of Dido and Aeneas 1957.

A meeting of the Old Students Association in 1955.

One of the highlights of the year was the school sports day when many a Witney athlete dreamed of Olympic stardom.

Mrs Early presenting the Inter-house sports cup to the Captains of 'Grocers' House', Margaret Warner and John Turner on July 14, 1951, held on the school sports field off Duckington Lane.

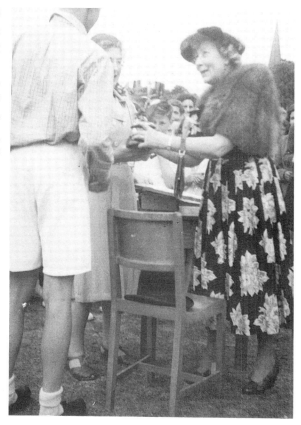

B. Bradley winning the 440 yards boys under 14 years in 1951 in 66.8 seconds. A school record.

Janet Read in the high jump for girls in 1951.

Girls relay race in 1951: Toni Whiteley, Gillian Smith, Carol Pether

Girls relay race 1951: Sybil Read and Rosemary Cook waiting for the baton.

Group photograph of a girls' House team on sports day 1951 taken on the Leys. Left to right: Sybil Read, Mary Read, Elizabeth ?, R. Palmer, P. Alexander, D. Pemberton, R. Crass, Rosemary Cook, Carol Pether, Gillian Smith, M. Gould, S. Prior, Mary Moffatt, P. Preston, C. Dafter, R. M. Ward.

Witney Grammar School Football Team 1904-5, names unknown.

# *The Witney Bombs*

In November of 1940, two bombs were dropped on Witney. One landed near Clinch's Brewery, the other outside St Mary's school in Church Green. Mrs Dorothy Hawkins (nee Florey) recalls. 'The planes came over about five in the morning. Two bombs were dropped on Church Green, but even in Bridge Street we felt the effect. A whole row of army lorries parked outside the Fleece were damaged and all the windows down to Market Square were smashed in. No one was hurt fortunately, but it made quite a mess. You can still see the crater marks now and where the shrapnel went into the walls.' Michael Druce, whose parents lived on Church Green, tells us, 'wooden shutters protecting the second floor windows, were blown in, landing on top of an oak wardrobe, just missing my parents lying in bed.' Mr Wally Honey, former Transport Manager at Clinch's Brewery, claims the bombs were not German. He found a detonator, which he claims was British, handing it over to the police. Yet a former German Burgomaster and ex-bomber pilot, has admitted responsiblity and has apologised to the town since. The dropping of the bombs could have been a mistake, being jetisoned over what was thought to be open country-side, having been caught in the bomb-bay of the bomber. Yet some believe a light from the brewery broke the blackout and the bomb-aimer thought below him was Leafield Radio Station. Perhaps we shall never know the truth.

Church Green after the bomb.

Clearing up after the bomb on Church Green.

An Oxford Mail photograph of Clinch's Brewery showing the bomb damage.

The Oxford Mail of Saturday 23rd November 1940, was published during the darkest days of the war when Britain stood alone against Germany and her Axis allies. Reports of raids on England never gave the location, Witney was referred to as 'a Home Counties town'. The front page contained four pictures of a 'Home Counties town'.

Old newspapers make fascinating reading and this four page edition of the Oxford Mail (newsprint was in short supply), contains some real gems. Vivian Leigh was appearing in *Waterloo Bridge* at the Ritz (Oxford) and Harry Welchman and Tessa Dean in *Maid of the Mountains* at the New Theatre, Oxford. The cheapest seat was 9d in the balcony (a little under 4p). Hartwells had a selection of cars for sale, notably a one year old Morris 8 for £135. Several people were fined for breaking the 'black-out' law but a cyclist was fined 5 shillings for not having a light ... how things change!

# SECTION FIVE

# *A Mystery Visitor?*

This photgraph has been in my collection for sometime but I have been unable to identify the event. One interesting suggestion is that it is a visit to Witney by the infamous Oswald Mosely ... but perhaps you know better!

# *Witney Fire Brigade*

Towards the end of the nineteenth century there had been several major fires in Witney, notably Early's mop factory, so mill owner William Smith formed the Witney Volunteer Fire Brigade. On 7, June 1880 he took delivery of a new horse-drawn fire engine costing £200 and placed it in Shuffrey's Barn in the High Street. There are stories of how the engine was kept there, while the horses were stabled at the other end of town. Leaving a lot to be desired for an efficient call-out. Often a fireman on a bicycle attended the fire first to see if it was worth calling out the brigade. All the volunteers then were businessmen and the usual method of call-out was to ring a special bell at his house. Or, as in one case, a telegram was sent. Yet surprisingly they did manage to control most of the fires.

Witney's first fire engine.

It was not long before the engine was moved to Millin's Yard in the High Street and in 1927 a second-hand 1915 Leyland motor machine was bought and the brigade moved to the Corn Exchange Yard. In 1937 a new Leyland engine was purchased at a cost of £900, and this has since been restored and is now kept at the brigade's present headquarters in Welch Way, which was opened in 1966. Up until 1936 the brigade was still run on a voluntary basis but control was handed over to the Witney Urban District Council about then, until after the war when Oxfordshire County Council took control. All retained firemen now have extensive training and have personal radios for call-out and can expect to attend a fire in Witney within ten minutes.

The 1936 Leyland Tiger Cub fire engine, now restored.

Later machines in use at Witney Fire Station.

Witney Volunteer Fire Brigade in 1910 The horses came from Payne's and normally pulled the Witney Station horse bus. The numbered people are: 1 Fred Middleton, 2 Bob Warner, 3 ?, 4 Stan Collier, 5 Hedley Vickers, 6 Sam Shuffrey, 7 ?, 8 John Rose, 9 Harry Broom, 10 Fred Green, 11 ?, 12 ?, 13 Will Payne, 14 Will Long.

Members of the brigade dressed up in old uniforms for the Tercentenary of Early's outside the mill in 1969. left to right: Cliff Russell, Bill Pilcher, Leo Hicks, Don Fidler, Gordon Skeates, Bill Godfrey, Cyril Godfrey, Dennis Robinson.

Restoring the 1936 Leyland engine, Cyril Godfrey (left) and Gordon Skeats (right).

The Witney brigade in 1937. Back row: P. Johnson, R. Vickers, J. Pickett, K. Rudge, J. Baker, W. Rotherham. Front row: CFO A. Valentine, R. Keates, A.E. Jones, R. Dingle, G. Wright H. Turner, T. Leigh.

The Witney brigade in 1983 relaxing after training. Top Row: R J. Fidler, A. Godfrey, S. Fletcher, S. Hare, N. Hamblin, M. Charlotte. Front Row: C. Barber, E. Godfrey, M. Jewell, B. Shepard, P. Godfrey.

The Witney brigade in 1976. The Tiger Cub had then been fitted with a much longer ladder. Top Row: B. Shepard, P. Harper, Roger Godfrey, Steve Fletcher, M. Charlotte, Finlayson, P. Godfrey, Mike French, Darrell Bayliss, Michael Pincher, E. Godfrey, S. Hare. Bottom Row: P. Linsay, Mervyn Jewell, Stn O. Cyril Godfrey, Sub O. Gordon Skeates, LF. George Houghton, LF. I. Marsden, LF. Bob Haley.

Station Officer Cyril Godfrey explains a point to firefighters Peter Godfrey and Paul Linsay after a drill at Zedcor's in 1982.

At the end of a pool marathon in aid of the Fire Service Benevolent Fund. Left to right: Andrew Godfrey, Michael Pincher, Herby Hare, Darrell Bayliss, Mervyn Jewell, Jim Collett.

## Fires

There have been several major fires in Witney since 1880. Notably the following:

>New Mills, 19 January 1883
>Saltmarsh and Druce, 22 November 1903
>Witney Mills, 11 January 1905
>Tarrant's Stores, 20 June 1911
>Pritchett's Gloves, 14 April 1926
>Witney Aerodrome, 1936
>Swan Laundry, 1937
>Witney Blanket Company, 1939
>Mount Mills, 13 April 1953
>Cook and Boggis, 17 December 1964
>Buttercross Works, 22 March 1968
>Newland Warehouse, 3 April 1975
>Swan Laundry, 22 October 1993
>The Woolgate Centre, 5 October 1998

On 11 January 1905 there was a major fire at Early's Mill, which left the factory gutted. Fortunately the Witney Volunteer Fire Brigade had already been formed by William Smith — actually a rival mill owner — and although their equipment was basic some of the mill was saved. For some unknown reason, Earlys celebrated the event on February 24 the same year with a four-course dinner held in the Temperance Hotel.

Fire at Witney Mill, January 1905.

The fire at Pritchett's Glove factory in Newland on 14 April 1926 caused a major row. As Newland was part of Coggs then and not Witney, allegedly the local brigade refused to turn out. Mr. Looker the manager entered the blazing building in order to call the Oxford brigade who arrived three-quarters of an hour later. Meanwhile the Witney brigade decided to turn up connecting their hose to a hydrant at Newland Blanket Warehouse. Unfortunately they soon discovered their hose was too short. Consequently, the factory was totally destroyed. At the height of the blaze it was so hot that chickens in a nearby hen house burst into flames, roasted alive.

The glove factory after it was rebuilt.

All hands to the pump in case of another fire?

Inside the glove factory in the 1930s.

Buttercross Works (now Poundstretcher's) well alight on 22 March 1968.

Leading Fireman Cyril Godfrey fights the Buttercross blaze helped by two firefighters from Banbury.

# *Witney Carnival*

One of the highlights of Witney's year is the carnival held on the Leys every July, proceeded by a procession of floats through the town. The annual event actually goes back to 1928 when it was sponsored by the British Legion and held on the King George's Recreation field at Newlands. It was much bigger in those days, with most of the firms as well as schools in the town decorating floats. During the Second World War, the carnival ceased for the duration. It was not until 1988 it was revived by the Witney Lions, Witney Round Table, the Rotary Club of Witney and Witney Rugby Club. To start with it was a very small affair held at Coggs, no more than a fete, but it soon moved to the Leys becoming a far greater event. In 1998 displays were given by the Sunrisers Marching Band, Giant Sumo Wrestlers, Strawberry Fayre Majorettes and the Solent Eagles Motorcycle Display Team, as well as a fun fair. The whole event, as in the past, is held for various charities. Unfortunately the procession through the town no longer attracts the entries it use to, now comprising mainly schools.

Eastern magic in 1928.

Black and White minstrels in 1930.

The procession going up Newlands in 1930.

Early's float leaving Newland warehouse in 1931.

Percy Brown (right foreground) preparing his motorcycle for an obstacle race at Witney Carnival 1931.

The Kodak girls from the glove factory at the carnival in 1930.

A touch of the orient from the glove factory girls in 1936.

School children advertising Witney's three Bs, bread, beer and blankets in 1932.

The Ramblers float in 1932.

More Carnival pictures from 1928.

The top photo is beleived to be from 1928 and the bottom 1930.

Early's at Newlands, preparing for the carnival in 1931.

Also taken in 1931 is this crowd scene, the photographer has clearly managed to gain their attention!

# Around Witney: The Buildings

The principal town of West Oxfordshire and the seat of the District Council, Witney was originally a Saxon town linked to the legend of Queen Emma, granddaughter of Rolle, Viking founder of Normandy. The Queen of both Aethelred the Unready and King Canute, her sons by each marriage, Edward the Confessor who was born at Islip and Hardcanute, becoming kings of England. Although there is no documentary evidence to support it, it is alleged she gave the Manor of Witney to the Bishops of Winchester in gratitude for being found not guilty by ordeal of the murder of her son Alfred and an affair with the Bishop. It is known she did witness the granting of Witney by Edward the Confessor to the See of Winchester. Emma's Dyke, a canalized stream draining an abandoned river-meander west of the town which runs beneath Corn Street to join the River Windrush at the Church of St. Mary, has no known connection to her.

Witney remained a part of the Winchester estates after the Norman Conquest and they developed it into a market centre. By 1279, although the town only had 255 tenants it had a market and two fairs — one of which became the present day Witney Feast. During the Black Death, Witney was drastically affected and over two-thirds of the population died. Wool and the making of cloth played an important part in the town's prosperity, and through it Witney developed into a wealthy Medieval town, but few buildings of that period remain — except the ruins of the Bishop's Palace at Church Green. Church Green, where the market place was once held is to a typical wedge-shape Middle Ages design, as is incidentally, the exact length of a Medieval archery pitch

Witney has been visited on numerous occasions by royalty. Saxon kings knew the area well but the first recorded visit was by John between 1207 to 1214, often staying at the Bishop's Palace. His son Henry III spent £20 on a new wardrobe of Witney cloth when he visited in 1221. Elizabeth I stayed at the White Hart Inn (then situated by Witney Bridge on the Windrush) on 16, September 1592 giving the inn a tapestry. King Charles I came to the town between 18 to 20 June 1644 and James II was presened with a pair of Witney blankets in 1688. Queen Anne probably knew the town well through her friendship with the Duchess of Marlborough. King George came to the town twice during the last war and our present Queen paid a royal visit on 8, April 1959 and her mother in 1960.

Most of the buildings in the centre of town are of Cotswold stone built in the eighteenth and nineteenth centuries and most now have preservation orders on them.

It is often claimed Witney's most famous building, the Buttercross, was built by William Blake, but on the site was once a statue of the Virgin Mary and in 1606 Richard Ashcome left £50 in his will to build a house over the cross and in 1683 William Blake gave a legacy for a clock and a cupola to the built over it. No one actually knows when the Town Hall opposite was built. There was certainly an assembly hall on the site during the middle seventeenth century to an advance design, which incorporated an open space beneath it acting as a corn market.

The War Memorial at the entrance to Church Green was dedicated on 12, September 1920. There are 144 names engraved on it from the First World War, often as many as three from the same family, such as Puckett, Horne and Miles with four members of the Long family. After the Second World War new plaques were added on which there are 32 names.

This post card of the Buttercross and Town Hall was sent by Herbert Phelps to his sister in Worcester at 6.45pm on October 21 1902. Note the stage coach!

Woodstock Road and Woodgreen in 1915. The message on the back to Flo Hawkes of 18 The Crofts reads: 'Dear Flo, What do you think of this? Don't you reckon it makes a very pretty picture, after all ours is a Charming little town, although we could do with a change could'nt we. With love from Liz.'

This photograph of the bridge at the juction with High Street and Bridge Street was taken during the Second World War.

This photograph of Mill Street looking east was taken in 1895 by Henry Taunt the Oxford photographer.

Newlands in the 1920-30s.

The Leys Walk in 1906. The trees were planted by Dr Augustine Batt in 1873 to hide the noise of the railway station.

Market Square in the early 1960's little changed. The concrete structure in front of the Eagle Vaults was the town air raid shelter for use in the Second World War.

The same view of Market Square in the late 1930s.

West End in the 1950s. The two pubs on the left are the Harriers and the Elm Tree.

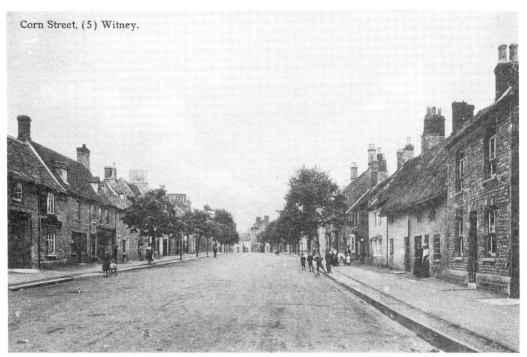

Corn Street, (5) Witney.

Corn Street in the 1890s. It looks so much wider without cars.

Witney Grammar School Avenue.

The parish church of St Mary's dominates the centre of Witney. An early Norman church during the Thirteenth Century the tower, simliar in design to that of Oxford Cathedral, was added and the church was almost entirely rebuilt with additions during the Fourteenth and Fifteenth Centuries showing the prosperity wool gave to the town. Between 1865-9 the church was somewhat over-restored by G.E. Street. Church Green which it faces, is designed almost like a cathedral close and is lined with Georgian and Victorian houses the former homes of merchants in the wool trade.

Witney Bridge and the Blanket Hall in about 1906. The pub on the right was the King's Arms and is now a furniture shop and the Windrush Club.

The Angel Inn, 1938.

ALWAYS
CONGENIALITY AND CONVIVIALITY
AT

# THE ANGEL INN

CLINCH'S PRIZE MEDAL BEERS
FULLY LICENSED

Excellent Accommodation                Free Car Park

## MARKET SQUARE
## WITNEY, OXON

Proprietor : R. H. Walker                Telephone 238

Since this photograph was taken this pub in Market Square has changed little – apart from it now has more flowers and the sign has been altered. In an the advert it claimed it had 'Congeniality and Conviviability' – and this can be said of the pub today. It also advertised Clinch's prize medal beers, excellent accommodation, and a free car park – although in reality this was probably outside in the road. The licensee at this time was R.H. Walker.

Witney High Street in about 1910. The building on the left was the Post Office. The building on the right by the cyclists in the middle of the road was Knight's printing works and the offices of the Gazette.

The Cross Keys, this photo of could easily have been taken yesterday, but was in fact taken in 1939. Then classed as an hotel it advertised accommodation for 'commercial gentlemen with bed and breakfast', had a car park and garages, gave personal attention with moderate charges. A Clinch pub the licensee was Thomas Cable.

A sight never seen today. Sheep grazing on Church Green in about 1905.

Holy Trinity Church on Woodgreen was designed by B. Ferry with an aisleless nave and built in 1849.

The original Tower Hill Garage built for the Thomas family by Boulton and Paul in 1928-9.

The West End Post Office and Fish and Chip Shop. The latter was previously the Jolly Tucker pub.

This building at the entrance to Church Green estate was once the fondly remembered Bull pub.

Originally built in 1703 and may have been called the Black Prince, it was sold in 1856 as the George. A stone and rubble building with internal walls of wattle and daub, it is now part of the offices and showrooms of Kernahan's Garage.

# Around Witney: The People

Until recently Witney was a relatively small market town and most residents worked in the blanket mills. As is common with most small towns generations of families have grown up and died here. Names still common in Witney can trace their roots back centuries. Such as Clack, Horne, Pratley, Wright, Fisher, Lomax, Druce, Payne, Marriott, Haynes, Blake, Keates and naturally Early.

Witney has now been designated an expansion town with the result many new people are moving into the area. New estates are developing on the outskirts of the town, one of the first being Smith's estate, part of which belonged to the Air Ministry and was used as service quarters. The Coggs estate which is a mixed development of private, council and housing association, as is the new estate at Deer Park. Thorney Leys was built in the 1980s and continues to grow with a new planned development at Coral Springs. Fortunately Witney is not becoming a dormitory town and most of the newcomers are integrating well, playing a full part in the economic and social life of Witney. Blanket making is no longer the main industry for the town has several industrial estates on its outskirts now.

Witney has an active social life, with most interests and hobbies catered for, from lace making to kick boxing to brass band and orchestral music. It also has twenty-two pubs, not including licensed social and sporting clubs — with another three planned, a nightclub, several high class restaurants, a leisure centre with a swimming pool, keep fit and bodybuilding gymnasia, the Corn Exchange now also acts a cinema, Langdale Hall holds dances, fairs and other large events, while the young of the town are not forgotten. There are several youth football and rugby sides catering from eight years old and up, and many go on to play semi-professionally in the larger local sides. Youth organisations such as the Scouts and the Boys Brigade still flourish in the town and recently a golf course was built at Downs Road and is actively encouraging membership.

Most Witney residents do their shopping in the town, with four supermarkets and now two shopping centres, the Woolgate and Wesley Walk, not including the many other shops, some of which have been established in the town for generations. Oxford, which is a thirty minute ride away is handy with buses every fifteen minutes, with connections there to London. But why travel there, when parking in the many town centre car parks is still free!

The Rhythmic Aces a popular dance band who played in Witney during the 1950s. All the members came from Witney. Ron Lomax (Bass) Jimmy Bridgman (Trumpet) Jimmy Mullins (Sax) Douglas Lomax (Drums) Don Haynes (Sax and Accordion) Stanley Horne (Piano)

Jack Prior (Coachman) on Walter Midwinter's cab in Farm Mill Lane in 1920.

Pupils at St Mary's School in about 1920. Back row: W. Keen, G. Warner, B. Keeling, W. Radburn, G. Broom, F. Clack. Middle row: G. Steptoe, ? Smith, H. Leach, B. Hosier, J. Harris, W. Rolls, W. Walker. Front row: A. Ford, J. Horn, P. Steptoe, T. Brooks, J. Rowls, C. Bustin, G. Gould, C. Gotobed, B. Townsend, W. Fox.

A later photograph taken in about 1957 of Miss Marsh leading her classes at St Mary's School onto Church Green for the annual May Pole dances. The blond-haired lad is Robert Bridgeman, while the other children include, Alice Early, John Warner, Trevor Hughes and Tim Brooks.

In St Mary's School yard in 1958. Left to right: John Taylor, Robert Bridgeman, Stanley Jenkins, Jane Keates, Wendy Allen, Malcolm Gotobed.

In 1939 Witney received many refuges from London. This photograph, taken outside the Rectory, Church Green shows Kathleen Jenkins visiting her son Stanley Edgar Jenkins. The picture also shows Mortimer Jenkins, (Stanly's elder brother) who was later posted to Witney as an NCO in the Royal Army Ordnance Corps attached to the Army Airborne Services at Broadwell.

The children of American Airforce Sergeant Mazarasso playing in Cresswell's Yard, 55 High Street in 1956. Left to right: Dolores Lorraine Mazarasso, Stanley Jenkins, Roy Mazarasso.

The Horne family outside the Eagle Tavern, Corn Street in about 1911.

Joining the Boy Scouts movement always was and still is popular organisation for the youth of Witney to join. This photograph taken in May 1937 outside Church House, Church Green. Many of those in the photograph are still alive and live in Witney. Back row: Norman Pritchard, ? Bruce, Ben Boughan, George Moss-Holland. Middle rows: ? Huggins, John Buckle, Tom Brown, Alan Dominey, Les Charlett, ? Rose, Richard Peace, Victor Delnevo, Fred Delnevo, Terry Phillips, Arthur Rose, ?, Ron Lomax, Doug Lomax, Leyland Coutts, ?, Dennis Boughan, Geoffrey Wells, ?, Ray Newell, John Paintin, John Hewett, Eddie Oliffe, John Baston, Dennis Cooper. The Cubs: David Littleford, ?, Mike Thomlinson, Gordon Keates, ?, Jimmy King, ?, Ron Keates, Colin Warner.

Workers from Marriott's Mill celebrating at the annual firm's dinner sometime in the 1950s. The photo was taken in the Masonic Hall, Church Green.

On the right of this photograph is Vera Langford (nee Green), with a friend at Smith's Bridge Street Mill in the 1930s.

Another photograph taken in the Masonic Hall. This one celebrating the coronation of George VI in May 1937.

When peace was declared in 1945, many areas of Witney held children's parties. The venue for this photograph is unknown.

The children from West End joining their Victory Party in 1945. This photograph was taken in the yard opposite the House of Windsor pub.

The Bull public house was famous for its darts team, winning many trophies during its day. Unfortunately the pub no longer exists. Left to right: George Cooper, George Townsend, Jack Miles, Roy Smith, Frank Clack, Gerald Woodcock.

Boys football has played a big part in their education. This photograph taken in 1988 shows the school team of the Blake C.E. Primary School who were runners-up in the Primary Schools Cup. Most of these lads also played for local boys club sides at the weekend, such as F.C. Mills and Tower Hill. All are now young men and some still play football for local teams. Back row: Ryan Clarke, Alex Komineck, Phillip Honey, Jonathan Tillson, Thomas Dracon, James Montgomery  Andrew Eaton Front Row Gavin Komineck Jonathan Reeves  Neil Maskell (Capt), Jamie Smith, Jonnie Smith.

Members of Witney Bowls Club 1914. As can be seen most were businessmen. Back row: ?, Mr Basford, Isaac Walker (Butcher), Mr Buckingham (Jeweller), Mr Crowther, Charlie Jackson (Blacksmith). Middle row: Dickie Jones, Jack Teagle, Albert Horn, Charlie Miles. Front row: ? (Post Office), Fred Ford.

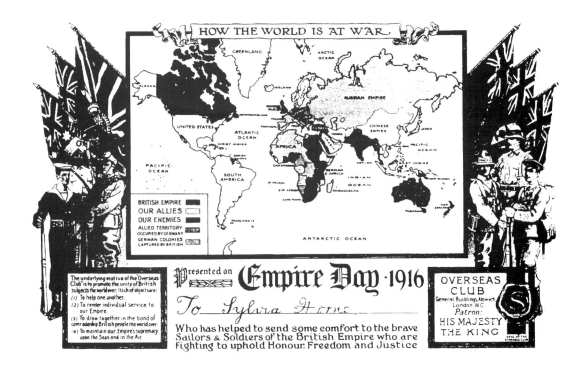

During the First World War the schoolchildren of Witney made small gifts, such as gloves and scarfs for the soldiers on the front. They were each presented with a certificate for their efforts.

John Clarke, 1851-1939

### The Clarke Family

John Clarke was a forceful and dynamic Witney character, who moved into building and property development by buying Spring Terrace, The Crofts, the buildings now occupied by the present and last post office — known as 'Elizabeth House' — and the site of what is now known as Highworth Place, which was then used as tennis courts. All this property was eventually sold off. He was also responsible for the development of the south side of Witney in 1899-1900, by erecting Leys Villas and parts of the Springs. The stones for the building of these homes came from a quarry which was situated where Spring Close is now. He also expanded the original ironmongers to trade as a timber and builders merchant, the latter of which still trades today off Welch Way. Sadly the ironmongers in the High Street was sold recently, but the name is preserved as Clarke's Restaurant.

John Clarke and his four daughters, Ginny (later Mrs Charles Griffin), Nell, Esther and Alice. The photo was taken in 1908 outside their home at Church View, The Leys.

The Clarke family taken at the Golden Wedding of John and Ellen Clarke in 1924. Back row: Charles Griffin, Nellie Clarke, William Clarke, Doris Clarke, Kenneth Wells, John Wells. Middle row: Nell Clarke, Ginny Griffin, Harry Clarke, John Clarke, Ellen Clarke, Hettie Clarke, Florence Clarke,  Alice Clarke. Front row: Marie Griffin, Roy Griffin, Monica Griffin, Mary Clarke, Barbara Clarke, Bernard Wells.

A view of the Clarke family home at Leys Villas in 1908.

William George Dossett was John Clarke's brother-in-law. They married the sisters Alice and Ellen Hudson whose father was a tailor with a shop where the Bradford and Bingley Building Society, High Street is today. William Dossett was born in 1958 at Kencott and was apprenticed to the grocery trade. In the early 1880s he worked for Saltmarsh and Druce as a traveller (company representative) and in 1887 he founded his own business in Banbury. Dossett and Co became Banbury's leading wholesale and retail grocer and wine merchant, not closing until 1973. Part of Banbury is still called Dossett corner'. In 1937 William Dossett retired back to Witney and bought a house on the Leys and near to his brother-in-law, John Clarke.

William and Alice Dossett with their two daughters, Gertrude and Mabel in 1901.

Roy Kinchen and John Dossett-Davies taken in 1943, both age 16 years in the uniform of Civil Defence messengers.

## National Savings

A National Savings Rally in the Market Square in 1943.

# *The Witney Railway*

The company was formed in 1859 to build a railway from Witney to Yarnton, thereby connecting the town to London, Oxford, Worcester and Wolverhampton. Set up by local businessmen with help from Clinch's Bank they included Charles Early, Henry Akers, Joseph Druce, William Payne, and Malachi Barlett, while local landowner Walter Strickland of Cokethorpe Park became its first Chairman. Sir Charles Fox was engaged to survey the route and although there was opposition from the Great Western and Midland Railway, an Act of Parliament was passed on 1st August 1859 granting permission. Work progressed well and on Wednesday 13th November 1861 the line was opened to passengers, the day declared a holiday in Witney.

For a while the line was worked by the West Midland Railway and when the East Gloucestershire line opened that company shared the station. This came to an end in 1890 when both companies were bought out by the G.W.R.

The first station was built to the rear of the church at Station Lane and the building was not pulled down until recently when it was part of Marriotts coal yard. The second station was opened on 15th January, 1873 with the main buildings on the up-platform with a small canopy; from 1925-30 the building was extended. Under Marple's regime on 16th June, 1962 the station was officially closed to passengers, although some trains still ran for a while after. In 1970 the goods yard ceased trading and in January 1969 the later station buildings were demolished, although for a while part of the platforms remained. Later the goods shed became the Sidings nightclub for a while, but now the

whole area is part of the Two Rivers Industrial Estate. Many Witney people can remember the station and line with affection and with the congestion now on the roads, with foresight perhaps, the closing of the line was not such a good idea. There has been talk of using the route as a road-rail, but much of the land has been taken over and only the remains of one bridge still exist, hidden in undergrowth in Witney Meadows Park.

These ladies were collecting for the Railways Benevolent Institution in 1918. Before they were excempt from service many railwaymen enlisted in the army and were killed. Before the introduction of the welfare state, widows and their children relied on charity to maintain them.

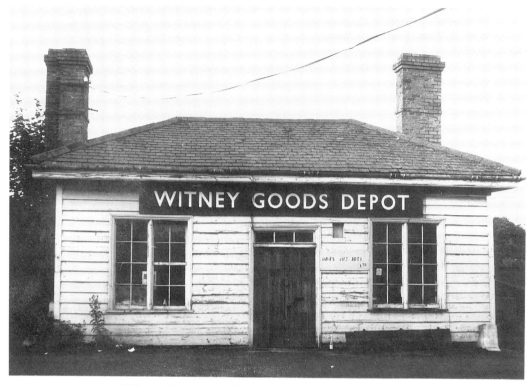

Witney Station in the 1930s. It changed little after.

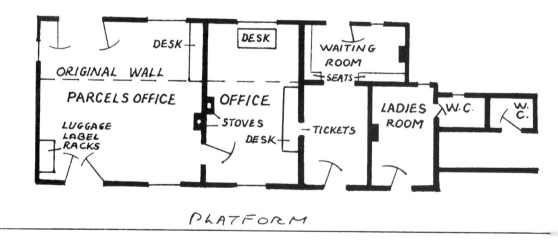

Plan of the station.

Witney station early this century, the train arriving is from Oxford.

Class 22 No 6332 draws slowly forwards into Witney 1861 station in order to collect a wagon load of industrial waste on Friday 30 December 1970

Right from the outset the railway proved very popular with Witney people. It gave them access to parts of the country not known before, and the Company actively encouraged this with regular daily excursions. Even in Victorian days trains of sixteen carriages long were common, packed with day trippers.

The more adventurous passenger could even go abroad. On 20, July 1933 a day trip was organised to Boulogne, France. Leaving at 5.10 am the whole fare costing 33/6d return. A day trip to Brighton in the same year cost 9/- return leaving at 7. 0am, while you could go on any train all day to Reading for only 3/- return. Football fans were well catered for also. Every Saturday trips were organised to First Division matches within an eighty mile radius.

Local market days were also catered for every Thursday as far back as 1897. An advert of the day stated:

---

### CHEAP TRAINS TO WITNEY
### Every THURSDAY, until further Notice

### MARKET TICKETS
will be issued to
### WITNEY

As under

| From | Forward Journey am | Fare 3rd Class s. d. | Time of Return from Witney |
|------|------|------|------|
| YARNTON | 9  19 | 1  2 | 3  14  and  7  20 |
| EYNSHAM | 9  26 | 0  8 | "        " |
| FAIRFORD | 10  30 | 2  0 | 5  7  and  9  40 |
| LECHLADE | 10  37 | 1  6 | "      " |
| ALVESCOT | 10  45 | 0  10 | "      " |
| BAMPTON | 10  52 | 0  6 | "      " |

The tickets are only available on the day of issue, and between the stations specified above; if used otherwise, the full Ordinary Fare will be charged.

---

A rare photograph of the last day of steam operation at Witney in December 1965. Clive Hepworth stands on loco 9973 while his friend Robert Viner looks on. Both were members of the Witney Grammar School Railway Club.

The original station which was acting as the goods depot in 1970.

Class 22 No D6328 diesel locomotive shunts at Witney in February 1970. Some goods sidings had already been lifted by then, and there was, by this time, little traffic other than coal.

Class 22 No 6328 collects empty 16 ton mineral waste wagons from the sidings at Witney on 13, February 1970.

The Witney Wanderer', the last passenger train out of Witney on 31, October 1970, arrives at the entrance to the goods yard. On the last day passengers jumped down onto the ballast in order to walk along the track into the 1861 station.

A return rail ticket Oxford-Witney, issued 26 March, 1941

# *Clinch's Brewery*

Lack of space prevents a full chapter in this book on the history of brewing and Witney pubs, but it is hoped to included further details in Changing Faces of Witney Book II. The tradition of brewing in Witney goes back many centuries — it is one of the three Bs, bread, beer and blankets - the town is famous for. As with most towns brewing started way-way back when the landlords of the various pubs and taverns brewed their own beer. Sometimes he found it more profitable to brew beer and to sell it on to other pubs, and from this the brewing industry started, reaching its height in the Nineteenth Century. One famous brewery, Brakespears of Henley actually started in a Witney pub — the Cross Keys — in this way.

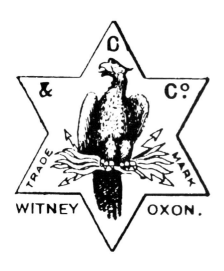

The most famous of Witney breweries was the Clinch Brewery on Church Green. Founded by John William Clinch, the son of a (Clinch's trade mark) banker, he first started brewing at Page Nine the Fleece Hotel on Church Green in 1811. Such was the popularity of his beer that in 1839 he purchased several run-down cottages on Church Green, demolished them and built a new brewery on the vacant plot. The actual date is disputed, for even in their centenary year book, published in 1939, the brewery claimed the company was started in 1841. In the past most breweries were built on or near a river, not only for the supply of water, but often to run the machinery inside. Unfortunately for John Clinch his new brewery did not have this facility, but he soon solved it. Not too far away was the River Windrush and a well down Skinner's Yard. This yard, still there, was down a lane directly opposite his brewery where Church Green ends and Market Square begins. So John dug a pipe line from his brewery to this well and pumped the water up from there.

In 1871 the founder died and he was succeeded by his son William until his death in 1891. A year later the brewery was formed into a limited company. The brewery were fortunate to have the backing of Clinch's Bank, for after the First World War, along with most of the country, the brewery felt the effect of the world-wide depression, and sales dropped off. It was the start of a long struggle to keep the company afloat. By then they owned 71 pubs from Witney through to Oxford and Swindon and were even selling beer to Birmingham and the Oxford colleges. It was these sales that really kept the company going, that and the appointment of L. B. Clark as head brewer who replaced John Welch. Clark was probably one of, if not the best, brewers in the country. Between 1929 to 1939 he won sixteen first prizes, two championship gold medals, seven second prizes and ten third prizes for his beer submitted at the annual competition at the Brewers Exhibition in London. He was a Diploma Member of the Institute of Brewing and under him Clinch's won first prize for its brown ale and second prize for its strong ale at the Brewers Exhibition in 1938. Between the wars the Managing Director was Tom Forshew who was related to the Clinchs by marriage, but after his son was killed during the Second World War he seemed to lose interest in the company.

By the nineteen-sixties the company was in deep financial trouble, only the selling off of a few pubs and help from the bank keeping them afloat. In 1962 an approach was made by Courage and accepted. The offer, £850,000, when compared with the £45m sell off Morrell's in Oxford in 1998, must amount to the biggest bargin of the century. As was expected, the brewery was closed down a year later, although it became a distribution centre for some time after. Courage, of course, were only interested in the assets and selling their beers through the pubs, and even today some of the old Clinch's pubs still sell it, despite having changed hands many times since. The Cross Keys still displays its Courage sign while being a Scottish and Newcastle pub.

In 1939 Clinch's owned fourteen pubs in Witney. The Three Horse Shoes, the Hollybush, the Nags Head, the Star (both now closed) all in Corn Street, the Angel, the Bull (now closed) and the Cross Keys in Market Square.The Carpenter's Arms at

Newland, the Three Pigeons on Woodgreen, King's Arms and the Prince of Wales in High Street (both now closed) the Royal Oak and the Plough, also in the High Street, as well as the Fleece on Church Green. Tom Forshew, the Managing Director also owned the Rosedean Hotel on Church Green, which he sold to the District Council as offices for £2,000 in 1936.

The site of the brewery is now the Church Green Industrial Estate, but the tradition of brewing continues in the old malting house, where with an entrance in the Crofts, the Wychwood Brewery brews its distinctive and popular beers.

The main part of Clinch's brewery.

The Malt House.

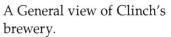

A General view of Clinch's brewery.

Internal view of the Malt House.

Fermenting Room

The bottle label of the award winning brown ale.

The Beer Cellar

Bottling Store

The Wine and Spirits Store

"From this bottle, I am sure
You'll get a glass both good and pure
In opposition to a-many
I'm striving hard to make a penny."

Old landlord's prayer